ANTIDUMPING POLICY

1. Introduction

Dumping, as defined most simply, is the sale of goods for export at a price below that available in the local market.[1] Economists have devoted much attention to analyzing dumping,[2] but they have paid little attention to analyzing antidumping policy.[3] This omission may have occurred because economists have found little reason to justify antidumping policy except in cases of predation. Ethier (1983), in describing a commonly-held view, asks "Why do countries have antidumping laws at all, since the opportunity to buy goods at a low price would seem to be a good thing." Hence, antidumping policy must be counterproductive since it raises the price of imports.

This view of antidumping policy, however, is not complete. By itself, a commitment to an antidumping policy may change strategic behavior in imperfectly competitive markets. We show in this paper that the mere threat of antidumping enforcement may change firm behavior in a manner that raises the home country's welfare. Strategic behavior is altered because, as it is typically administered, an antidumping policy represents a credible threat to impose future duties based on the current price differential between home and foreign markets. Firms have incentive to manipulate this price differential

---

[1] See Viner (1923) and Wares (1977).

[2] See Viner (1923), Yntema (1928), and Haberler (1937). More recent treatments include Wares (1977), Ethier (1982), Davies and McGuinness (1982), Brander and Krugman (1983), Gruenspecht (1988), and Lahiri and Sheen (1990).

[3] For exceptions, see Dixit (1988), Fischer (1990), Prusa (1991), and Staiger (1991). Gruenspecht (1988) considers a prohibition on dumping, which differs from the current practice of imposing antidumping duties.

in the event that dumping is ultimately punished. These manipulations may produce positive or negative welfare effects, depending on the strategic variable. It is even possible that the foreign country may benefit from the home country's antidumping policy.

We examine a three-stage, two-period model where a foreign firm is a monopolist in the foreign market, but competes with a native firm in the home market. When there is no antidumping policy, the increased competition in the home market implies that the foreign firm sets its export price below its local price. The game commences with the policymaker in the home country choosing the probability that dumping will be punished. Dumping in the first period is punished by the imposition of "antidumping" duties in the second period, where these duties equal the first-period price differential between home and foreign markets.[4] Since punishment occurs later, firm behavior in the first period is affected only by the threat of antidumping enforcement.

Under quantity competition, the threat of antidumping enforcement causes firms to alter their outputs in a manner that often improves the home country's welfare. In fact, this threat may lead to lower prices in the home market. Given that the actual imposition of duties may also improve the home country's welfare, a commitment to an antidumping policy frequently benefits the home country.

The threat of antidumping enforcement may also improve the foreign country's welfare, and the likelihood of this outcome increases as foreign consumption rises relative to foreign exports. Since the actual imposition of duties is harmful to foreign welfare, the overall impact of an antidumping

---

[4] Hence, firms can influence the size of antidumping duties, but not the probability of antidumping enforcement. Prusa (1991) and Fischer (1990) develop models where firms affect the probability of enforcement.

2

policy on foreign welfare may be either positive or negative.

Under price competition, a commitment to an antidumping policy produces vastly different results. The imposition of antidumping duties can overwhelm the home firm's cost disadvantage, or improve its cost advantage, thereby creating significant changes in pricing behavior. A commitment to an antidumping policy worsens welfare in the home country, unless the home firm is at a large cost disadvantage relative to the foreign firm. In addition, this policy frequently lowers welfare in the foreign country.

We also examine whether the above results hold in the case of imperfect substitutes. Although these findings are not substantively changed under quantity competition, they are altered under price competition because the foreign country <u>always benefits</u> from price changes caused by the <u>threat</u> of antidumping enforcement.

The effects of antidumping policy become more involved if the game is extended to more than two periods. In a multiperiod Bertrand game, an antidumping policy may cause the foreign firm to engage in hit-and-run export behavior. Moreover, this policy may also encourage entry by home firms which is beneficial to the home country's welfare.

Our paper is organized as follows. Section 2 presents the model for the Cournot case. Section 3 presents the Bertrand case. Section 4 relates our model to the case of imperfect substitutes. Section 5 offers concluding remarks.

2.   The Cournot Case

A multiperiod game would be a natural starting point for modelling firm behavior under antidumping policy. To simplify the analysis, we examine a three-stage, two-period duopoly model. The game starts with a commitment by the policymaker, who chooses the extent to which she will punish dumping. Let $I_t = 1$ if dumping in period t is punished by the imposition of antidumping duties in period $t+1$. These duties equal the dumping margin [i.e., the difference between prices in the home and foreign markets] in period t.[5] Otherwise, $I_t = 0$ if dumping in period t is not punished. The policymaker selects $\theta = \mathrm{Prob}(I_t = 1)$.[6] After θ is announced, firms choose their first-period outputs. If dumping is punished, duties are imposed prior to the second output period. This period concludes the game. Since antidumping duties are <u>not</u> in effect in the first period, but <u>an antidumping policy may be in effect</u>, the welfare results in this period illustrate the

---

[5] This assumption conforms most closely with the actual administration of antidumping statutes in the European Community and the United States [see Wares (1977) and Vakerics, Wilson, and Weigel (1987)]. Under U.S. law only, firms can request an annual review of dumping duties based on recent pricing behavior. If firms stop dumping, or if the dumping margin becomes smaller, a portion of the originally-collected duties may be refunded. Nevertheless, several sources have indicated that the original dumping duties often remain in effect for a substantial period because reviews are not requested [presumably due to high costs of collecting and assembling price information]. Also, a backlog frequently arises that inhibits the timely performance of reviews. Under E.C. law, there is no process whereby dumping margins are regularly reviewed.
Even if dumping could be monitored closely, and duties frequently adjusted, firms would still have the same strategic incentives that they display in the first period of our model. For instance, assume that dumping is always discovered and punished in the same period that it occurs. Dumping would still occur with positive probability, and firms would still manipulate the dumping margin through their output choices [see footnote 11].

[6] We can obtain qualitatively similar results by instead assuming that dumping is always punished, and that <u>partially-offsetting</u> antidumping duties are enforced. In this case, θ represents the portion of the dumping margin that is offset by a duty.

strategic behavior that arises from the <u>threat of antidumping enforcement</u>.

By assumption, one foreign firm and one home firm compete in the home market. They produce perfect substitutes. Through a cost advantage, or imposed trade restraints, the foreign firm is a monopolist in its own market. Since the two markets are separable, the intensified competition in the home market causes the foreign firm's export price to be lower than its local price. In the application of many antidumping statutes, this type of discriminatory pricing is treated as dumping.

We solve for a subgame-perfect Nash equilibrium, assuming that firms use Cournot conjectures in setting their outputs. Each firm faces a constant marginal cost, which equals $c_t(C_t)$ for the home(foreign) firm at time t.[7] The inverse demand functions for the home and foreign markets are, respectively, p^t and P^t. Also, h_t and H_t respectively denote the home firm's and foreign firm's outputs for the home market, while F_t denotes the foreign firm's output for the foreign market.

In period t, the home firm's profits are

$$\pi^t = [p^t(h_t+H_t) - c_t]h_t. \tag{1}$$

Similarly, the foreign firm's export profits are[8]

$$\Pi^t = [p^t(h_t+H_t) - C_t - I_{t-1}s_{t-1}]H_t, \tag{2}$$

where s_{t-1} is the dumping margin from the prior period. Hence,

$$s_{t-1} = s^{t-1}(F_{t-1},h_{t-1},H_{t-1}) = \max[0, P^{t-1}(F_{t-1}) - p^{t-1}(h_{t-1}+H_{t-1})]. \tag{3}$$

_____

[7] **Capital** letters denote foreign variables. Our results are scarcely affected by relaxing the assumption of constant marginal costs.

[8] Without loss of generality, we let transportation costs equal zero. We treat dumping duties as a tax to the foreign firm, even though they are paid by the importer. Of course, the importer may be a distribution arm of the foreign firm. With unaffiliated perfectly-competitive importers [and constant returns to scale in distribution], the price that the importer is willing to pay is exactly reduced by the magnitude of the imposed duties.

We can also describe the foreign firm's local profits,

$$\Pi*^t = [P^t(F_t) - C_t]F_t. \tag{4}$$

Solving by backward induction, we derive the output equilibrium in the home market in the second period. The first-order conditions are:

$$\partial\pi^2/\partial h_2 = p^2 + p^2{}'h_2 - c_t = 0; \quad \partial\Pi^2/\partial H_2 = p^2 + p^2{}'H_2 - C_t - I_1 s_1 = 0, \tag{5}$$

where ' indicates the first derivative of the inverse demand function. As shown in the following conditions, we assume that marginal revenue is declining with respect to a firm's own output and its rival's output:[9]

$$\partial^2\pi^t/\partial h_t \partial h_t = 2p^t{}' + p^t{}''h_t < 0; \quad \partial^2\Pi^t/\partial H_t \partial H_t = 2p^t{}' + p^t{}''H_t < 0 \tag{6}$$

$$\partial^2\pi^t/\partial h_t \partial H_t = p^t{}' + p^t{}''h_t < 0; \quad \partial^2\Pi^t/\partial H_t \partial h_t = p^t{}' + p^t{}''H_t < 0. \tag{7}$$

Given the above conditions, a unique second-period Cournot-Nash equilibrium will exist for each value of $I_1 s_1$ [associated with an internal equilibria]. Let $h_{2N}(I_1 s_1)$ and $H_{2N}(I_1 s_1)$ represent these equilibrium output levels. When dumping in the first period is punished [i.e., $I_1 = 1$], a change in the first-period dumping margin has the following effect on second-period outputs:

$$\partial h_{2N}/\partial s_1 |_{I_1=1} = -(\partial^2\pi^2/\partial h_2 \partial H_2)/A > 0$$

$$\partial H_{2N}/\partial s_1 |_{I_1=1} = (\partial^2\pi^2/\partial h_2 \partial h_2)/A < 0 \tag{8}$$

where $A = (\partial^2\pi^2/\partial h_2 \partial h_2)(\partial^2\Pi^2/\partial H_2 \partial H_2) - (\partial^2\pi^2/\partial h_2 \partial H_2)(\partial^2\Pi^2/\partial H_2 \partial h_2) > 0$.

If dumping is punished, an increase in the dumping margin in the first period raises the imposed duties on the foreign firm in the second period. Consequently, home output increases and foreign output decreases in the second period.

Let $\pi^{2N}(I_1 s_1)$ and $\Pi^{2N}(I_1 s_1)$ describe each firm's profits in the home

---

[9] These conditions represent the second derivatives of each firm's profit function in period t. They ensure a stable second-period equilibrium, and also a stable first-period equilibrium when $\theta = 0$.

market in the second-period Cournot-Nash equilibrium. When dumping in the first period is punished, an increase in the first-period dumping margin has the following effect on second-period profits:

$$\partial \pi^{2N}/\partial s_1 |_{I_1=1} = p^{2\prime}h_{2N}(\partial H_{2N}/\partial s_1)$$
$$= p^{2\prime}h_{2N}[(\partial^2\pi^2/\partial h_2 \partial h_2)/A] > 0$$

$$\partial \Pi^{2N}/\partial s_1 |_{I_1=1} = -H_{2N} + p^{2\prime}H_{2N}(\partial h_{2N}/\partial s_1)$$
$$= -H_{2N}[1 + (p^{2\prime}(\partial^2\pi^2/\partial h_2 \partial H_2)/A)] < 0 \tag{9}$$

If dumping is punished, an increase in the dumping margin in the first period results in higher profits for the home firm and lower profits for the foreign firm in the second period. For notational convenience, $\partial \pi^{2N}/\partial s_1$ and $\partial \Pi^{2N}/\partial s_1$ will hereafter refer to $\partial \pi^{2N}/\partial s_1 |_{I_1=1}$ and $\partial \Pi^{2N}/\partial s_1 |_{I_1=1}$.

Having solved the second-period problem,[10] we now move to the first-period problem. In this period, the home firm maximizes its profits by solving,

$$\max_{h_1} \pi = \pi^1(F_1, h_1, H_1) + \lambda\theta\pi^{2N}(s^1(F_1, h_1, H_1)) + \lambda(1-\theta)\pi^{2N}(0), \tag{10}$$

where λ is the discount factor. The home firm knows that any dumping during the first period will be punished with probability θ, and that future antidumping duties will be imposed based on the first-period dumping margin. Equation (10) leads to the following first-order condition:

$$\partial \pi/\partial h_1 = \partial \pi^1/\partial h_1 + \lambda\theta(\partial \pi^{2N}/\partial s_1)(ds_1/dh_1) = 0. \tag{11}$$

Given that $s^1(F_1, h_1, H_1) > 0$, it holds from (3) that $ds_1/dh_1 = -p^{1\prime} > 0$. Hence, $(\partial \pi^{2N}/\partial s_1)(ds_1/dh_1) = -p^{1\prime}(\partial \pi^{2N}/\partial s_1) > 0$. By increasing its output in the first period, the home firm raises its profits in the second period when

---

[10] Based on our prior assumptions, the foreign firm maximizes second-period profits in its local market by choosing the output level that solves $\partial \Pi*^2(F_2)/\partial F_2 = 0$. This value of F_2 uniquely maximizes $\Pi*^2(F_2)$.

an antidumping policy is in effect. An output increase by the home firm causes price to fall in the home market in the first period, which increases the dumping margin. If dumping is punished, this action leads to higher antidumping duties in the second period, and the home firm reaps higher profits in that period. Hence, the policymaker's commitment to an antidumping policy provides incentive for the home firm to boost its first-period output.

Turning to the foreign firm's first-period problem, analagous reasoning shows that the following first-order conditions must be satisfied:

$$\partial \Pi / \partial H_1 = \partial \Pi^1 / \partial H_1 + \lambda \theta (\partial \Pi^{2N} / \partial s_1)(ds_1/dH_1) = 0 \qquad (12)$$

$$\partial \Pi / \partial F_1 = \partial \Pi^{*1} / \partial F_1 + \lambda \theta (\partial \Pi^{2N} / \partial s_1)(ds_1/dF_1) = 0. \qquad (13)$$

Given that $s^1(F_1, h_1, H_1) > 0$, it holds from (3) that $ds_1/dH_1 = -p^{1\prime} > 0$ and $ds_1/dF_1 = P^{1\prime} < 0$. Thus, $(\partial \Pi^{2N} / \partial s_1)(ds_1/dH_1) = -p^{1\prime}(\partial \Pi^{2N} / \partial s_1) < 0$ and $(\partial \Pi^{2N} / \partial s_1)(ds_1/dF_1) = P^{1\prime}(\partial \Pi^{2N} / \partial s_1) > 0$. Under an antidumping policy, an increase in foreign exports in the first period reduces foreign profits in the second period. By increasing its exports, the foreign firm lowers the first-period price in the home market, and thus _raises_ the dumping margin. If dumping is punished, this action leads to higher antidumping duties and lower foreign profits in the second period. In contrast, by increasing locally-consumed output in the first period, the foreign firm lowers price in the foreign market. This action _lowers_ the dumping margin, and raises foreign profits in the second period under antidumping enforcement. Hence, the policymaker's commitment to an antidumping policy provides incentive for the foreign firm to reduce exports and increase locally-consumed output in the first period.

For the forthcoming analysis, we assume that competitive conditions

8

lead to lower prices at home than abroad in the absence of an antidumping policy. Letting $F_{1N}(\theta)$, $h_{1N}(\theta)$, and $H_{1N}(\theta)$ represent equilibrium output levels in the first period, this assumption implies that $s^1(F_{1N}(0), h_{1N}(0), H_{1N}(0)) > 0$. We can now totally differentiate the first-order conditions in equations (11)-(13), and evaluate at $\theta = 0$:[11]

$$dh_{1N}/d\theta|_{\theta=0} = (\lambda p^{1\prime}/A)[(\partial\pi^{2N}/\partial s_1)(\partial^2\Pi^1/\partial H_1\partial H_1)$$
$$- (\partial\Pi^{2N}/\partial s_1)(\partial^2\pi^1/\partial h_1\partial H_1)] > 0,$$

$$dH_{1N}/d\theta|_{\theta=0} = (\lambda p^{1\prime}/A)[-(\partial\pi^{2N}/\partial s_1)(\partial^2\Pi^1/\partial H_1\partial h_1)$$
$$+ (\partial\Pi^{2N}/\partial s_1)(\partial^2\pi^1/\partial h_1\partial h_1)] < 0,$$

$$dF_{1N}/d\theta|_{\theta=0} = -\lambda P^{1\prime}(\partial\Pi^{2N}/\partial s_1)/(\partial^2\Pi^{*1}/\partial F_1\partial F_1) > 0. \qquad (14)$$

We conclude that:

---

[11] For purposes of our analysis, an __antidumping policy__ represents a commitment that dumping will be punished with positive probability. Hence, the effects of an antidumping policy are represented by a marginal increase in θ from zero.

   As θ increases further, two interesting results arise: (1) dumping is never eliminated completely, and (2) a __mixed-strategy equilibrium__ may arise. The intuition behind these results is as follows. From (11), it holds that $\partial\pi/\partial h_1 = \partial\pi^1/\partial h_1 + \lambda\theta(\partial\pi^{2N}/\partial s_1)(ds_1/dh_1)$. Letting $h_1^o(F_1, H_1)$ represent the value of h_1 that solves $P^1(F_1) - p^1(h_1 + H_1) = 0$, it holds that $s^1(F_1, h_1, H_1)$ =(>) 0 if h_1 <(>) h_1^o. Hence, $\lambda\theta(\partial\pi^{2N}/\partial s_1)(ds_1/dh_1)$ =(>) 0 if h_1 <(>) h_1^o. This result implies that $\partial\pi/\partial h_1$ is discontinuous, with an upward jump at h_1^o. Based on this behavior, the home firm has two possible profit-maximizing strategies: (i) act "nonstrategically" and refrain from using output to manipulate the dumping margin [i.e., h_1 solves $\partial\pi^1/\partial h_1 = 0$], or (ii) act "strategically" and use output to increase the dumping margin [i.e., h_1 solves $\partial\pi^1/\partial h_1 + \lambda\theta(\partial\pi^{2N}/\partial s_1)(ds_1/dh_1) = 0$, where $\lambda\theta(\partial\pi^{2N}/\partial s_1)(ds_1/dh_1) > 0$]. If the home firm acts "nonstrategically", and so does the foreign firm, then each firm sets the same output that it would in the absence of an antidumping policy. Hence, dumping occurs, and each firm is acting nonoptimally. Thus, strategy (i) can never be used in a pure-strategy equilibrium. Strategy (ii) can be used in a pure-strategy equilibrium, or as part of a mixed-strategy equilibrium [in conjunction with strategy (i)]. Under strategy (ii), dumping necessarily occurs.

<u>Proposition 1</u>: An antidumping policy raises home output, lowers foreign exports, and raises foreign consumption in the first period.[12]

As shown below, the reduction in foreign exports may not exceed the increase in home output. Hence, <u>the threat of antidumping enforcement</u> may increase home consumption. In other words, the home country may benefit from <u>lower</u> prices due to the <u>threat</u> of antidumping enforcement:[13]

<u>Lemma 1</u>: An antidumping policy lowers(does not change, raises) the first-period price in the home country if $\partial \pi^{2N}/\partial s_1 > (=, <) |\partial \Pi^{2N}/\partial s_1|$.

<u>Proposition 2</u>: Assume that demand is linear [i.e., $p^{t''} = 0$] and stable [i.e., $p^t = p$ for all t]. An antidumping policy <u>lowers</u> the first-period price in the home country if the foreign firm's share of the home market is less than 1/3.[14]

Proof: Refer to (14), and consider $d(h_{1N}+H_{1N})/d\theta$. Using (6) and (7), it follows that $d(h_{1N}+H_{1N})/d\theta = (\lambda(p^{1'})^2/A)[\partial \pi^{2N}/\partial s_1 + \partial \Pi^{2N}/\partial s_1]$. Given that

---

[12] Referring to (14) and (9), these output effects increase in size as h_{2N} and H_{2N} become larger. Hence, ceteris paribus, as demand grows in the second period, a commitment to antidumping enforcement has a greater impact on first-period output choices.

[13] The threat of antidumping enforcement provides the home firm with an incentive to increase its output in order to raise the size of subsequent dumping duties. Moreover, the home firm's output response becomes greater as its market share grows [since a given increase in duties has a larger effect on the home firm's profits]. If the home firm's market share is sufficiently large, its output response swamps that of the foreign firm. Thus, price falls in the home market.

By itself, a fall in the first-period price in the home market raises the dumping margin. This effect is counterbalanced, since the price decrease in the foreign market lowers the dumping margin.

[14] Foreign market share is that share which exists when a duty is imposed equal to the "original" dumping margin [i.e., the dumping margin in the absence of an antidumping policy].

$(\lambda(p^{1\prime})^2/A) > 0$, it holds that $d(h_{1N}+H_{1N})/d\theta \gtreqless 0$ if $\partial \pi^{2N}/\partial s_1 + \partial \Pi^{2N}/\partial s_1 \gtreqless 0$ [i.e, if $\partial \pi^{2N}/\partial s_1 \gtreqless |\partial \Pi^{2N}/\partial s_1|$]. If demand is linear, then $\partial \pi^{2N}/\partial s_1 + \partial \Pi^{2N}/\partial s_1 = (2/3)[h_{2N} - 2H_{2N}]$. This expression is positive if $h_{2N} > 2H_{2N}$ [i.e., if the foreign firm's market share is less than 1/3]. QED

The above results can be used to evaluate the impact of an antidumping policy on first-period welfare.[15] Welfare is measured as the aggregation of producer surplus and consumer surplus [and government revenue]. Hence, the home country's welfare in the first period is:

$$w^1 = \pi^1 + \int_0^{h_1+H_1} p^1(z) \; dz - p^1(h_1+H_1)$$

$$= (p^1 - c_1)h_1 + \int_0^{h_1+H_1} p^1(z) \; dz - p^1(h_1+H_1) \qquad (15)$$

We differentiate w^1 with respect to θ:[16]

$$dw^1/d\theta \big|_{\theta=0} = -p^{1\prime}[h_{1N}(dh_{1N}/d\theta) + H_{1N}(d(h_{1N}+H_{1N})/d\theta)]$$

$$= -p^{1\prime}(h_{1N}+H_{1N})[(dh_{1N}/d\theta) + \Phi_1(dH_{1N}/d\theta)], \qquad (16)$$

where $\Phi_1 = H_{1N}/(h_{1N}+H_{1N})$ [i.e., the foreign firm's share of the home market in the first period]

Consider (16). Noting that $-p^{1\prime}(h_{1N}+H_{1N}) > 0$, $dh_{1N}/d\theta > 0$, and $dH_{1N}/d\theta < 0$,

---

[15] The first-period welfare results in our model are of the most interest since firms realize that their behavior in this period may affect future antidumping duties. These "strategic" considerations are absent in the second period, which finishes the game. Of course, if our finite-horizon game were extended to more than two periods, "strategic" considerations would arise in every period except the last one. Considering a longer game would not change our qualitative results significantly.

[16] In deriving the result below, we note that $h_{1N}(0)$ solves $\partial \pi^1/\partial h_1 = 0$ [i.e., $p^1-c_1 = -p^{1\prime}h_{1N}$]. Without an antidumping policy, output choices in the first period are independent of conditions in the second period.

we obtain:

Lemma 2:   An antidumping policy raises(does not change, lowers) the home country's welfare in the first period if $\Phi_1 <(=,>) -(dh_{1N}/d\theta)/(dH_{1N}/d\theta)$.

From (16), it also holds that as $\Phi_1 \Rightarrow 0$, $dw^1/d\theta \Rightarrow -p^{1\prime}(h_{1N}+H_{1N})(dh_{1N}/d\theta) > 0$. From this result, we conclude:

Remark 1:   If the foreign firm's share of the home market is "sufficiently small", then an antidumping policy raises the home country's welfare in the first period.

By substituting (14) into (16), we obtain:

$$dw^1/d\theta\big|_{\theta=0} = [\lambda(p^{1\prime})^2(h_{1N}+H_{1N})/A] \text{ X}$$

$$((\partial\pi^{2N}/\partial s_1)[-(\partial^2\Pi^1/\partial H_1\partial H_1) + \Phi_1(\partial^2\Pi^1/\partial H_1\partial h_1)]$$

$$+ (\partial\Pi^{2N}/\partial s_1)[(\partial^2\pi^1/\partial h_1\partial H_1) - \Phi_1(\partial^2\pi^1/\partial h_1\partial h_1)]). \qquad (17)$$

Consider (17). Note that $\lambda(p^{1\prime})^2(h_{1N}+H_{1N})/A > 0$. It can also be shown that $(\partial\pi^{2N}/\partial s_1)[-(\partial^2\Pi^1/\partial H_1\partial H_1) + \Phi_1(\partial^2\Pi^1/\partial H_1\partial h_1)] > 0.$[17] Given these results, and that $\partial\Pi^{2N}/\partial s_1 < 0$, it holds that $dw^1/d\theta\big|_{\theta=0} > 0$ if $[(\partial^2\pi^1/\partial h_1\partial H_1)-\Phi_1(\partial^2\pi^1/\partial h_1\partial h_1)] \le 0$. Thus, a <u>sufficient</u> condition for welfare to increase in the first period is that:

$$(\partial^2\pi^1/\partial h_1\partial H_1) - \Phi_1(\partial^2\pi^1/\partial h_1\partial h_1) = (1-2\Phi_1)p^{1\prime} + (1-\Phi_1)p^{1\prime\prime}h_{1N} \le 0. \qquad (18)$$

From the above, it follows directly that:

Proposition 3:   Let demand be either linear or concave [i.e., $p^{t\prime\prime} \le 0$].

---

[17] From (6) and (7), $\partial^2\Pi^1/\partial H_1\partial H_1 = 2p^{1\prime} + p^{1\prime\prime}H_1 < 0$ and $\partial^2\Pi^1/\partial H_1\partial h_1 = p^{1\prime} + p^{1\prime\prime}H_1 < 0$. Since $0 \le \Phi_1 \le 1$ and $\partial^2\Pi^1/\partial H_1\partial h_1 < 0$, we obtain: $-(\partial^2\Pi^1/\partial H_1\partial H_1) + \Phi_1(\partial^2\Pi^1/\partial H_1\partial h_1) \ge -(\partial^2\Pi^1/\partial H_1\partial H_1) + (\partial^2\Pi^1/\partial H_1\partial h_1) = -p^{1\prime} > 0$.

12

An antidumping policy raises the home country's welfare in the first period whenever the foreign firm's share of the home market is 1/2 or less.

Since Proposition 3 provides only a sufficient condition, an antidumping policy may improve the home country's welfare in the first period even if the foreign firm's market share is significantly greater than one half.

A commitment to an antidumping policy causes the home firm to boost its first-period output in order to increase any imposed antidumping duty. This increase in output raises the home country's welfare, since the home-market price exceeds the home firm's marginal cost. An offsetting welfare effect may occur, however, because the foreign firm reduces its first-period exports [in order to lower any imposed duty]. By itself, this action raises prices in the home country, but part of this consumer loss is merely a transfer to the home firm. The home country, though, does not recover any lost consumer surplus that arises when consumers of foreign exports pay higher prices. If the foreign firm's share of the home market is sufficiently small, this loss is swamped by the efficiency gains resulting from increased home production.[18] Accordingly, the home country's welfare improves in the first period. From this analysis, we observe that the <u>home country frequently benefits from threatened antidumping enforcement.</u>

Next, consider the foreign country's first-period welfare:

$$W^1 = \Pi^1 + \Pi\star^1 + \int_0^{F_1} P^1(z) \; dz - P^1(F^1)$$

---

[18] Consumers of foreign exports may actually gain, however, because the threat of antidumping enforcement can cause price to fall [see Proposition 2].

13

$$= (p^1 - C_1)H_1 + (P^1 - C_1)F_1 + \int_0^{F_1} P^1(z)\,dz - P^1 F_1. \tag{19}$$

Differentiating with respect to θ, and evaluating at $\theta = 0$, we obtain:

$$dW^1/d\theta \big|_{\theta=0} = p^{1\prime} H_{1N}(dh_{1N}/d\theta) - P^{1\prime} F_{1N}(dF_{1N}/d\theta)$$

$$= H_{1N}[p^{1\prime}(dh_{1N}/d\theta) - \mu_1 P^{1\prime}(dF_{1N}/d\theta)], \tag{20}$$

where $\mu_1 = F_{1N}/H_{1N}$ [i.e., the (first-period) ratio of foreign consumption to foreign exports in the absence of an antidumping policy].

Consider (20). Noting that $p^{1\prime}, P^{1\prime} < 0$ and $dh_{1N}/d\theta, dF_{1N}/d\theta > 0$, we obtain:

Lemma 3: An antidumping policy raises(does not change, lowers) the foreign country's welfare in the first period if $\mu_1 >(=,<) p^{1\prime}(dh_{1N}/d\theta)/P^{1\prime}(dF_{1N}/d\theta)$.

To lower antidumping duties in the event that dumping is punished, the foreign firm boosts output for local consumption in the first period. This action raises the foreign country's welfare since the local price is above the foreign firm's marginal cost. In contrast, foreign welfare is negatively affected by the decline in foreign export profits [due to increased output by the home firm]. As foreign consumption increases relative to foreign exports, this welfare loss is eventually swamped.

Ex ante, the above propositions describe the first-period welfare effects that arise from an antidumping policy. Ex post, these results describe the overall welfare effects that arise if dumping was not punished. A commitment to an antidumping policy may raise overall welfare in both countries.

14

Of course, the threat of antidumping enforcement is credible because the policymaker commits to imposing antidumping duties with positive probability. The actual imposition of antidumping duties produces welfare effects similar to those arising from the imposition of an import tariff. Prior literature [see Brander and Spencer (1984) and Eaton and Grossman (1986)] has shown that imposing an import tariff improves the home country's welfare in a Cournot oligopoly with home and foreign firms. Thus, unless the antidumping duties are overly large, the home country also benefits in the second period from an antidumping policy.[19] We presume that if the foreign firm's share of the home market is small, then an antidumping policy often raises the home country's overall welfare. Moreover, this policy may still improve welfare when the foreign market share is large.

The foreign country suffers a welfare loss from the imposition of antidumping duties in the second period, since its export profits decline. This loss may overwhelm any welfare gain in the first period. As foreign consumption increases relative to foreign exports, the foreign country is more likely to benefit overall from the home country's commitment to an antidumping policy.

3.   The Bertrand Case

We now assume that firms set prices instead of quantities, and use Bertrand conjectures. Under our price-setting assumption, the home firm cannot influence the price received by the foreign firm in the home market.

---

[19] When θ represents the portion of the dumping margin that is offset by a duty [see footnote 6], a marginal increase in θ from zero will increase the home country's welfare in the second period. The output and welfare effects in the first period are very similar to those described above.

Hence, a commitment to an antidumping policy does not change the "strategic" nature of the home firm's behavior. As we shall show, the foreign firm may continue to act strategically depending on the size of its cost advantage. Welfare results depend on which firm possesses a cost advantage, and in some cases, the magnitude of the cost advantage.

Under Bertrand behavior with perfectly substitutable goods, a given firm has incentive to undercut its rival's price whenever that price exceeds its marginal cost. If one firm has a cost advantage over another firm, the equilibrium price equals the marginal cost of the high-cost firm, and the low-cost firm serves the entire market.[20] When both firms face the same marginal cost, the equilibrium price equals that marginal cost. Any division of market shares is compatible with equilibrium.

Suppose that both firms face the same costs before any trade policies are imposed, i.e., $c_t = C_t = k_t$ for all t. In the absence of an antidumping policy, the equilibrium price in the home market equals k_t in period t. The price in the foreign market, $P\!*_t$, is set at the monopoly level, $P\!*_{tM}$, which solves $\partial \Pi\!*^t(P\!*_t)/\partial P\!*_t = 0$ [where $\Pi\!*^t = (P\!*_t - C_t)D^t(P\!*_t)$, and $D^t(P\!*_t)$ is the demand function for the foreign market]. Note that $P\!*_{tM} > k_t$.

Let the policymaker commit to an antidumping policy. In equilibrium, the first-period price in the home market must still equal k_1, and the first-period price in the foreign market must still equal $P\!*_{1M}$. If dumping is

---

[20] We assume that the consumers buy from the low-cost firm. Otherwise, an ϵ-equilibrium exists where the low-cost firm charges ϵ below the marginal cost of the high-cost firm.

Since its profits equal zero, one might wonder whether the high-cost firm should enter the industry. If entry decisions are made prior to the price-setting stage, it is a weakly dominant strategy for the high-cost firm to enter the industry in the absence of sunk costs. The implications of positive sunk costs are discussed later.

punished, the foreign firm must pay an antidumping duty of $P^*_{1M} - k_1$ during the second period. Since antidumping enforcement has conveyed an artificial cost advantage upon the home firm, the equilibrium second-period price in the home market becomes $k_2 + (P^*_{1M} - k_1)$ [or p_{2M}, where p_{2M} is the monopoly price level].[21] The home firm now serves the entire home market, but antidumping enforcement has succeeded in raising price above k_2 in the second period. Hence, the home country's welfare declines in the second period, which implies that it declines overall. Foreign welfare is unaffected because with or without an antidumping policy, foreign export profits equal zero in each period, and the local foreign price is at the monopoly level in each period.

Similar qualitative results are obtained if the foreign firm's cost of serving the home market exceeds the home firm's cost. We conclude that:

Proposition 4: If the foreign firm does not have a cost advantage in serving the home market, then an antidumping policy lowers the home country's welfare and does not affect the foreign country's welfare.

Now suppose that the foreign firm's cost of serving the home market is less than the home firm's cost, and also suppose that cost conditions are unchanged across periods. Hence, $c_t = k$ and $C_t = K$, where $k > K$. We also assume that the home firm's costs are less than the monopoly price level in the foreign market, i.e., $k < P^*_{tM}$ for all t.

Consider initially the case where $k \geq (K + P^*_{1M})/2$. In equilibrium under an antidumping policy, the foreign firm sets its first-period export

---

[21] If demand and cost conditions are identical in the two markets, and identical across periods, then antidumping enforcement does cause the home-market price to reach the monopoly level.

price, P_1, at k, and captures the home market.[22] This strategy minimizes the dumping margin, since the foreign firm charges the highest possible export price that still allows it to serve the market.

The foreign firm could set its first-period local price at $P*_{1M}$, which would result in a dumping margin of $P*_{1M}$ - k. If antidumping duties were imposed, then the foreign firm's export cost would equal $K + (P*_{1M}-k)$ in the second period. Having assumed that $k \geq (K+P*_{1M})/2$, it follows that $K + (P*_{1M}-k) \leq k$. We conclude that when the foreign firm sets its local price at or below the monopoly level in the first period, then it still possesses a cost advantage in the second period even if dumping is punished. Hence, the foreign firm's optimal strategy is to always maintain its cost advantage in the home market in the second period. Based on this result, the foreign firm maximizes profits by setting its local price in the first period at $P*_{1N}$, which solves[23]

$$\partial\Pi*^1(P*_1)/\partial P*_1 + \lambda\theta(\partial\Pi^2(s_1)/\partial s_1) = 0. \tag{21}$$

Given that the foreign firm has a cost advantage in the second period, the equilibrium price in the home market equals k in that period. It must hold that $\Pi^2(s_1) = (k - K - s_1)d^2(k)$, where d^2 is the second-period demand function for the home market. We obtain $\partial\Pi^2(s_1)/\partial s_1 = -d^2(k) < 0$. Hence, it

---

[22] We presume that k is below the foreign firm's monopoly price level in the home market.

[23] Antidumping duties equal zero until the foreign local price reaches k. However, optimal behavior requires that the foreign firm sets its local price at or above k [since $\partial\Pi*^1(k)/\partial P*_1 > 0$ for $P*_1 < k < P*_{1M}$, it holds that $\Pi*^1(k) > \Pi*^1(P*_1)$ for $P*_1 < k$]. Thus, in equilibrium, the dumping margin can be expressed as $s_1 = \max[0, P*_1-k] = P*_1-k$. From this, $ds_1/dP*_1 = 1$. Based on the above, the first-order condition for the optimal local price is (21).

follows from (21) that $P*_{1N} < P*_{1M}$.[24]   In order to lower any subsequent duties, the foreign firm reduces its local price below the monopoly level in the first period.

Since an antidumping policy leads to a price reduction in the foreign market, the foreign country's welfare increases in the first period.   The home country's welfare is unaffected in the first period because the home-market price remains at k.

The home-market price also remains at k in the second period; however, the home country now collects antidumping duties with positive probability. Accordingly, the home country's welfare increases in the second period, which implies that it increases overall.   Due to the payment of antidumping duties, the foreign country's welfare decreases in the second period.[25]   Hence, we conclude that:

Proposition 5:   Assume that costs are constant over time, and that the foreign firm has a cost advantage in serving the home market.   Let $k \geq$ $(K+P*_{1M})/2$, where k(K) is the home(foreign) firm's marginal cost, and $P*_{1M}$ is the monopoly price level in the foreign market in the first period.   A commitment to an antidumping policy raises the home country's overall welfare, raises the foreign country's first-period welfare, and lowers the foreign country's second-period welfare.

Finally, consider the case where $k < (K+P*_{1M})/2$.   In equilibrium under

----

[24] It is possible that $P*_{1N}$ does not exist, in which case the foreign firm sets $P*_1$ at k.   This occurs if $\partial\Pi*^1(P*_1)/\partial P*_1 + \lambda\theta(\partial\Pi^2(s_1)/\partial s_1) < 0$ as $P*_1 \Rightarrow k^+$.   Since $\partial\Pi^2(s_1)/\partial s_1 = -d^2(k)$, the necessary and sufficient condition for this outcome is $\partial\Pi*^1(k)/\partial P*_1 - \lambda\theta d^2(k) < 0$.

[25] In the second period, the local foreign price remains at $P*_{2M}$ under an antidumping policy.

an antidumping policy, the foreign firm still sets its export price at k in the first period, and captures the entire home market. However, in order to maintain a cost advantage in the <u>second</u> period under antidumping enforcement, the foreign firm must now set its local price below $P*_{1M}$ in the <u>first</u> period.

Let $P*_{1T}$ represent the value of $P*_1$ that solves $K + (P*_1 - k) = k$. Hence, $P*_{1T} = 2k - K$. If the foreign firm sets its local price at $P*_{1T}$ and its export price at k in the <u>first</u> period, then its export costs in the <u>second</u> period would equal k under antidumping enforcement.[26] To gain a cost advantage in the second period under antidumping enforcement, the foreign firm must sets its local price below $P*_{1T}$ in the first period. It may or may not be a profit-maximizing strategy to set price in this range, since the foreign firm sacrifices first-period profits by reducing price below $P*_{1M}$.

If it is a profit-maximizing strategy for the foreign firm to preserve its cost advantage in the home market in the <u>second period</u>, then the foreign firm sets its <u>local</u> price in the <u>first period</u> at $P*_{1N}$.[27] Thus, the welfare results are similar to those in Proposition 5.

If it is not a profit-maximizing strategy for the foreign firm to preserve its cost advantage, then optimal behavior requires that the foreign firm sets its local price at $P*_{1M}$ in the first period. As $k \Rightarrow K^+$, this behavior must represent the equilibrium outcome.[28] In the event of

---

[26] If the foreign export price equals k in the first period, then antidumping duties equal $P*_1 - k$. In this case, foreign export costs in the second period equal $K + (P*_1 - k)$ under antidumping enforcement. If $P*_1 = P*_{1T} = 2k - K$, then $K + (P*_1 - k) = k$. Note that $P*_{1T} < P*_{1M}$, given that $k < (K + P*_{1M})/2$.

[27] Alternatively, the foreign firm sets its export price at k [see footnote 24].

[28] To preserve its cost advantage in the second period in the event that antidumping duties are imposed, the foreign firm must set its local price below $P*_{1T}$ in the first period. If it foregoes its cost advantage, the

20

antidumping enforcement, the home firm serves the entire home market in the second period, and sets price at either $K + (P*_{1M} - k)$ or p_{2M}. Both of these prices exceed k, which is the second-period price in the absence of an antidumping policy.

Hence, as $k \Rightarrow K^+$, the effect of an antidumping policy is to increase the second-period price in the home market. The home country's welfare declines in the second period, which implies that it declines overall. Under these conditions, an antidumping policy also lowers the foreign country's welfare by reducing its export profits in the second period. We conclude as follows:

Proposition 6: Assume that costs are constant over time, and that the foreign firm has a cost advantage in serving the home market. Let $k < (K+P*_{1M})/2$. An antidumping policy either leads to the welfare results in Proposition 5, or it lowers welfare in both countries. As $k \Rightarrow K^+$, an antidumping policy necessarily lowers welfare in both countries.

We can use this last example, where the home firm is at a slight cost disadvantage, to illustrate the importance of antidumping policy to the entry decisions of firms. Since antidumping duties can override any innate cost advantage possessed by the foreign firm, an antidumping policy may create a profit opportunity for the home firm that induces entry.

---

foreign firm instead sets its local price at $P*_{1M}$ in the first period. Thus, the expression, $\Pi*^1(P*_{1M}) - \Pi*^1(P*_{1T})$, describes the minimum gain in first-period profits that arises if the foreign firm foregoes its second-period cost advantage. As $k \Rightarrow K^+$, $\Pi*^1(P*_{1M}) - \Pi*^1(P*_{1T}) \Rightarrow \Pi*^1(P*_{1M}) > 0$ [since, as $k \Rightarrow K^+$, $P*_{1T} \Rightarrow K^+$ and $\Pi*^1(P*_{1T}) = (P*_{1T}-K)D(P*_{1T}) \Rightarrow 0^+$]. However, by foregoing its cost advantage, the foreign firm loses profits in the second period. The maximum loss in second-period profits equals $\Pi^2(k,K) = (k-K)d(k)$. As $k \Rightarrow K^+$, $\Pi^2(k,K) \Rightarrow 0$. Hence, as $k \Rightarrow K^+$, the best strategy is to forego the second-period cost advantage.

Once again, let $k > K$. Let each firm incur the same entry cost, f, and assume that $(k - K)d^t(k) > f$ [where d^t is the home country's demand function in period t]. Consider a game where firms make simultaneous entry decisions after the policymaker commits to θ. In an equilibrium without an antidumping policy [i.e., $\theta = 0$], only the foreign firm enters the home market. If the home firm also enters, then Bertrand price competition causes price to fall to k. The home firm loses f overall, while the foreign firm still earns $(k - K)d^t(k) > f$ in each period. Equilibrium behavior requires that the foreign firm act as a monopolist in the home market; it sets the home-market price at the monopoly level, p_{tM}, in each period.

Now consider the effects of an antidumping policy [i.e., $\theta > 0$]. Let $k \Rightarrow K^+$. If the home firm decides to enter the market, then the foreign firm's optimal strategy is to forego its cost advantage in the second period in the event of antidumping enforcement. The foreign firm sets its export price at k and its local price at P^*_{1M} in the first period. Based on this behavior, the home firm would set its second-period price at $K + (P^*_{1M} - k)$ [or p_{2M}], and earn minimum second-period profits of $\lambda\theta(K+P^*_{1M}-2k)d^2(K+P^*_{1M}-k)$. If these profits exceed f, then the home firm's optimal strategy is to enter the market. An antidumping policy raises the home country's welfare in this case, because the home-market price falls from p_{1M} to k in the first period, and from p_{2M} to $K + (P^*_{1M} - k)$ in the second period. Also, positive profits are earned by the home firm. Foreign welfare declines because foreign export profits decline in both periods.

Remark 2: An antidumping policy may lead to entry. If it does, the home country's welfare increases and the foreign country's welfare decreases.

The above analysis shows that when the foreign firm has a relatively small cost advantage, an antidumping policy causes that firm to serve the entire home market in one period, and then disappear due to high dumping duties in the next period. If the game consists of more than two periods, then the foreign firm desires to serve the home market intermittently.

Consider a three-period game, and assume that demand and cost conditions are stable across all periods. Let $k > K$. As $k \Rightarrow K^+$, the foreign firm's equilibrium strategy under an antidumping polcy is to maintain a cost advantage in serving the home market in the first and third periods [see Appendix]. The foreign firm captures the home market in those periods only, while the home firm captures the home market in the second period. The price in the home market equals k in the first and third periods, and it approaches P^*_M in the second period, where P^*_M is the monopoly price level in the _foreign_ market. The price in the foreign market approaches P^*_M in all periods.[29] Once again, an antidumping policy is welfare-worsening for the home country.[30]

4.   Imperfect Substitutes

In this section, we offer some brief remarks concerning the effects of an antidumping policy when firms produce imperfect substitutes. Under

---

[29] Hence, as $k \Rightarrow K^+$, equilibrium pricing behavior approaches the result obtained when firms face identical costs.

[30] An antidumping policy raises the home market price above k in the second period, which reduces the home country's welfare. Consider the foreign country's welfare. An antidumping policy causes the foreign firm to raise its local price in the first period and to lower its local price in the second period [see Appendix]. Also, foreign export profits decline in the second period because the foreign firm loses its cost advantage. On balance, an antidumping policy would typically reduce foreign welfare.

Bertrand competition with imperfect substitutes, it can be readily shown that an antidumping policy raises the foreign export price and lowers the foreign local price in the first period.[31] This behavior serves to reduce any future antidumping duties. Since prices are strategic complements under typical demand assumptions, the increase in the foreign export price induces the home firm to raise its price in the first period. This action by the home firm increases foreign export profits, thereby improving the foreign country's welfare. The drop in the foreign local price also improves the foreign country's welfare. Thus, we obtain:[32]

Proposition 7: When prices are strategic complements, an antidumping policy raises foreign welfare in the first period.

When firms produce imperfect substitutes and engage in price competition, an antidumping policy may often improve the foreign country's overall welfare.

This result contrasts to that obtained in the quantity-setting case, where the imposition of an antidumping policy creates a strategic incentive for the home firm to raise output in the first period. This behavior induces a decline in foreign export profits. This effect may be strong enough to overwhelm the positive welfare effect that arises from the policy-induced increase in foreign consumption.

With either quantity-setting or price-setting behavior, an antidumping policy may raise the home country's welfare. In both cases, the home firm's output increases in the first period, which generates efficiency gains. In the price-setting case, however, an antidumping policy creates no incentive

---

[31] Proof available from author.

[32] Proof available from author.

for the home firm to act strategically. The home firm's output increases in the first period because the foreign firm raises its export price, thereby increasing demand for the home firm's product.

5.   Concluding Remarks

The above results show that an antidumping policy must be considered in light of its strategic effects. Depending on the nature of strategic behavior among firms, an antidumping policy may either improve or worsen the welfare of each country. Thus, it may be difficult to assess the overall welfare impact of a "blanket" antidumping policy that is applied uniformly to all product markets. Moreover, policymakers may have incentives to "fine-tune" the enforcement of antidumping statutes based on the prevailing competitive behavior in each product market. Given that it often difficult to empirically assess competitive conditions, a policymaker has plenty of latitude to make errors. Moreover, in the absence of procedures that lessen agency problems between firms and the policymaker, the process of selectively administering an antidumping policy would be susceptible to unproductive lobbying activities.

Our results also indicate that antidumping policy may be used as a type of "competition" policy. In quantity-setting oligopolies, the threat of antidumping enforcement provides direct incentives for home firms to aggressively expand their output. In general, an antidumping policy may induce entry by home firms that reduces the market power of foreign exporters.

Appendix

Consider the imposition of an antidumping policy in a three-period game. We assume that demand and cost conditions are stable across periods; hence, the profit functions remain unchanged over time. We express the home firm's profit function in period t as $\pi^t = \pi^o$. Similarly, the foreign firm's export profits are $\Pi^t = \Pi^o$ and its local profits are $\Pi*^t = \Pi*^o$ in period t. Finally, we assume that k > K, and examine behavior as $k \Rightarrow K^+$.

Since k > K, the foreign firm has a cost advantage in period 1. If the foreign firm has a cost advantage in period 2, [i.e., $k > K + s_1$, where $s_1 = \max(0, P*_1 - P_1)$], then the foreign firm will set its second-period prices so that it foregoes its cost advantage in period 3 [see footnote 28]. Given this result, the foreign firm's strategy can be analyzed in terms of three possibilities relating to its cost advantage in its export market: (a) maintain a cost advantage in period 1 only, (b) maintain a cost advantage in periods 1 and 2, and (c) maintain a cost advantage in periods 1 and 3. We show that (a) dominates (b), and that (c) dominates (a). Hence, (c) is the best strategy.

Under strategy (a), the foreign firm does not constrain its local price in order to maintain a cost advantage in periods 2 and 3. Hence, the foreign firm sets its local price at the monopoly level, $P*_M$, in all three periods. With antidumping enforcment, total foreign profits are $\Pi^a = (1+\lambda+\lambda^2)\Pi*^o(P*_M) + \Pi^o(k-K)$. As $k \Rightarrow K^+$, it holds that $\Pi^a \Rightarrow (1+\lambda+\lambda^2)\Pi*^o(P*_M)$ [because $\Pi^o(k-K) = (k-K)d^o(k) \Rightarrow 0$].

Under strategy (b), the foreign firm must constrain its local price in period 1 in order to maintain a cost advantage in period 2. The local price in period 1 cannot exceed $P*_{1T} = 2k - K$ [see text discussion]. The foreign firm sets its local price at $P*_M$ in periods 2 and 3, since it is unconcerned about maintaining its cost advantage. Thus, local foreign profits cannot exceed $\Pi*^o(P*_{1T}) + (\lambda+\lambda^2)\Pi*^o(P*_M)$ under strategy (b). Since the foreign firm only has a cost advantage in the first two periods, its export profits cannot exceed $(1+\lambda)\Pi^o(k-K)$ under strategy (b). Hence, total profits cannot exceed $\Pi^b = \Pi*^o(P*_{1T}) + (\lambda+\lambda^2)\Pi*^o(P*_M) + (1+\lambda)\Pi^o(k-K)$. As $k \Rightarrow K^+$, $\Pi^b \Rightarrow (\lambda+\lambda^2)\Pi*^o(P*_M)$ [because $\Pi*^o(P*_{1T}) \Rightarrow 0$ and $\Pi^o(k-K) \Rightarrow 0$]. Using this result and our previous result, it holds that as $k \Rightarrow K^+$, $\Pi^a - \Pi^b \Rightarrow \Pi*^o(P*_M) > 0$.

From the above, there exists $\epsilon > 0$, such that $\Pi^a > \Pi^b$ for $K < k < K+\epsilon$. Thus, strategy (a) dominates strategy (b) when k lies within this range. Now, consider strategy (a) again. Under this strategy, the foreign firm's export cost [and its equilibrium price] in the second period is $K + s_1 = K + (P*_M - k)$. Further, the foreign firm's export cost in the third period is $K + s_2 = K + (P*_2 - P_2) = k + (P*_2 - P*_M)$ [since $P_2 = K + (P*_M - k)$]. Thus, the foreign firm enjoys a cost advantage(disadvantage) in the third period if $P*_2 < (>) P*_M$. Hence, we can describe $\partial\Pi/\partial P*_2$ as follows,

$$\partial\Pi(P*_2)/\partial P*_2 = \partial\Pi*^2(P*_2)/\partial P*_2 + \lambda\theta\partial\Pi^3(s_2)/\partial s_2 \quad \text{for } [k <] \; P*_2 < P*_M,$$
$$= \partial\Pi*^2(P*_2)/\partial P*_2 \quad \text{for } P*_2 > P*_M,$$

Note that $\partial\Pi^3(s_2)/\partial s_2 = -d^o(k) < 0$, that $\partial\Pi*^2(P*_M)/\partial P*_2 = 0$, and that $\partial\Pi*(P*_2)/\partial P*_2$ is lower semicontinuous at $P*_M$. Hence, there exists $\tau > 0$ such that $\partial\Pi(P*_2)/\partial P*_2 < 0$ for $P*_M - \tau < P*_2 < P*_M$. By the mean-value theorem, $\Pi(P*_M - \tau) > \Pi(P*_M) = \Pi^a$. The foreign firm can earn higher profits by setting its local price below $P*_M$ in period 2, thereby maintaining its cost advantage

26

in period 3. Hence, strategy (c) dominates strategy (a). It can be readily shown that as $k \Rightarrow K^+$, the foreign firm's local price approaches $P\!*_M$ in all three periods.

References

Brander, James A. and Krugman, Paul R., "A 'Reciprocal Dumping' Model of International Trade," Journal of International Economics, November 1983, 15, 313-322.

Brander, James A. and Spencer, Barbara J. "Tariff Protection and Imperfect Competition," in H. Kierzkowski, ed., Monopolistic Competition and International Trade, Oxford: Clarendon Press, 1984, 194-206.

Davies, Stephen W. and McGuinness, Anthony J., "Dumping at Less than Marginal Cost," Journal of International Economics, February 1982, 12, 169-182.

Dixit, Avinash K., "Anti-Dumping and Countervailing Duties under Oligopoly," European Economic Review, 1988, 32, 55-68.

Eaton, Jonathan and Grossman, Gene M., "Optimal Trade and Industrial Policy under Oligopoly," Quarterly Journal of Economics, May 1986, 101, 383-406.

Ethier, Wilfred J., "Dumping," Journal of Political Economy, 1982, 90, 487-506.

_____, Modern International Economics, New York: W.W. Norton, 1983.

Fischer, Ronald D., "Endogenous Probability of Protection and Firm Behavior," mimeo, University of Virginia, 1990.

Gruenspecht, Howard K., "Dumping and Dynamic Competition," Journal of International Economics, February 1988, 25, 225-248.

Haberler, Gottfried von, The Theory of International Trade with its Applications to Commercial Policy, New York: Macmillan, 1937.

Lahiri, Sajal and Sheen, Jeffrey, "On Optimal Dumping," Economic Journal, Conference 1990, 100, pp. 127-136.

Prusa, Thomas J., "Antidumping Law and Firm Behavior," mimeo, SUNY-Stony Brook, 1991.

Staiger, Robert W. and Wolak, Frank A., "Strategic Use of Antidumping Law to Enforce Tacit International Collusion," mimeo, Stanford University, 1991.

Vakerics, Thomas V., Wilson, David I., and Weigel, Kenneth G., Antidumping, Countervailing Duty, and Other Trade Actions, New York: Practising Law Institute, 1987.

Viner, Jacob, Dumping: A Problem in International Trade, Chicago: University of Chicago Press, 1923.

Wares, William A., _The Theory of Dumping and American Commercial Policy_,
Lexington: D.C. Heath, 1977.

Yntema, Theodore O., "The Influence of Dumping on Monopoly Price," _Journal of
Political Economy_, December 1928, 36, 686-698.

www.ingramcontent.com/pod-product-compliance
Lightning Source LLC
Chambersburg PA
CBHW081317180526
45170CB00007B/2751